The Gift of Form:
A Pocket Guide to Formal
Poetry

John Brantingham

Spout Hill Press

Second Edition

May 2015

Copyright ©2015 by John Brantingham.
Individual poems copyright © the named poet.

spouthillpress.com
San Dimas, California

Cover design by Ann Brantingham

ISBN 10: 0692451307
ISBN 13: 978-0692451304

The Gift of Form:
A Pocket Guide to Formal
Poetry

John Brantingham

for Annie

Contents

Introduction

I used to have the same misconception about writing formal poetry a lot of people have. It scared me, and I didn't understand why there were so many arbitrary rules everyone had to follow.

It seemed to me that the rules would hurt the poetry. If I were caught up in trying to capture the meter and rhyme scheme, I would lose the sense of my overall idea.

I had a complete misunderstanding of what formal poetry was.

Then a few years ago, I decided to try out some formal poem types just for the fun of it. I thought the rules would offer me an interesting intellectual challenge and struggling against these restrictions would allow me to create interesting concepts.

I was still wrong. I still had a complete misunderstanding of what formal poetry was.

That summer, my challenge was to write a hundred sonnets. What I found in the course of that summer was that sonnets were not difficult or painful to write. They are challenging of course, but all poetry is.

As the summer moved along, I found that some of the difficulties I'd faced as a free verse poet were made much easier by the form. I had far less trouble with writer's block because the form actually draws ideas out of the writer. The first line suggests the last line and all the lines in between. I needed only to start the first line, and soon, I'd have the poem.

And then I made my largest intellectual shift: the rules of formal poetry are not there to be restrictions, and in fact there are not really any rules at all. After all, there are no poetry police. These are not rules but tools that help poets to move through a concept and the worst thing that would happen if I failed at writing my sonnet was that I'd end up with a good free verse poem.

I don't pretend that my insight was brilliant or new. Formal poets had known this for years, but it did change the way I approach poetry. I still write free verse, but I do so for other reasons.

When I have an idea about a theme or an idea that I want to express, I generally write it in free verse. When I don't have any idea about what I want to write, I follow a form. Free verse allows me to take an idea and shape it to my vision. Formal poetry draws out ideas I never knew that I had.

My epiphany about formal poetry created six basic premises about how and why to write it. These premises are also the premises of this book:

1. Writing formal poetry is intellectual game play. It should be fun.
2. Formal poetry gives poets tools that help them to say something meaningful.
3. No one can really fail at writing a formal poem. When poets break out of form, they simply have stopped writing in form and started to write free verse.

4. Writing formal poetry strengthens poets' and writers' free verse and prose.
5. A formal poem does not have to sound like an old poem. Modern themes, insights, and ways of speaking are perfectly acceptable. In fact, the job of poets is at least in part to write meaningfully about their time.
6. A poet should never have to sacrifice meaning to stay inside the form.

Again, these aren't the most surprising insights, but if you've never written a formal poem because you've been intimidated by them, you should feel a little relieved right now. Everything that seems intimidating about the sonnet, the villanelle, or the sestina should seem less so now.

Formal poetry not only is easier than you think it is, it actually will draw ideas out of you that you never knew you had.

Disclaimer

This is only a guide. Although I might make pronouncements about poetry, any advice in creative writing can be broken. There are no real hard and fast rules. If something works, even if it breaks the conventions of writing, it works. So follow this advice as far as you would like to do so. In fact, as you will find in all writing, any rule that you hear is just advice about what has worked or not worked in the past. What you might be doing is different and better. Follow your own instincts rather than slavishly following some idea you know isn't working for your poem.

Kindle and Nook Warning

If you are using a Kindle, Nook, or other similar device, rotate your screen so you have a landscape view. Otherwise, the lines of longer poems will be broken in strange places, ruining the effect and meaning of the poem.

Chapter One – Writing from the Body

Good poets were all first good readers of poetry. Why would people write poems after all if they didn't already love them? There is often a confusion however when people start writing. The job of a poet is different than the job of a reader.

Readers interpret themes, create meanings, understand symbols, and understand the overall point of the work of literature. For the most part, poets should not be focused on these concepts.

Good poets write action, physical sensation, and characters. There is a danger in trying to write a love poem or a hate poem. Often, when writers are caught up using abstract words, they lose the meaning and passion that drove them to write. The reason they use these words is that what they remember from their favorite poets is that those poet wrote about love or hate.

Go back and read your favorite poets. Notice that even when Shakespeare or Wordsworth or Seamus Heaney writes about love, they generally don't use the word "love." They're not writing essays after all. They're writing poems. The great poets are able to make us feel love. They do that by describing the physical sensations of people who are in love.

It is then the job of the reader to figure out what it means, and in fact different readers will often come away with different meanings to great poems.

This idea has many exceptions, and I'm sure you can find great poems that do exactly what I'm saying not to do. However, when you are just starting to write formal poetry or any poetry for that matter, you are going to find a lot more power in the poem that is merely physical and does not delve into abstract concepts at all.

All of those abstract concepts will be there, but they do not need to be explained. If we live in your body for a moment and feel what you feel and do what you do, we will understand your themes.

Following is a free verse poem called "Maternity Leave" by T. Anders Carson:

Maternity Leave

Lying in a heap.
Eating chocolates until noon.
Not lifting a finger in the kitchen.
Refusing to do dishes.
Full control of the remote.
Forgetting to buy groceries.
Forgetting the keys to the house.
Forgetting almost everything
and that's just the father to be.

Notice that he never explains his theme, and instead just develops a description of his character's life. He leaves the creation of theme to us, the readers. Because he has written his poem in this way, the theme becomes personal and complex. In fact, because he has not explicitly stated the theme, we might draw out any number of themes such as "men can be lazy," "pregnancy is a strange time of waiting," "life before parenthood is much different than after," or any number of themes. On top of everything else, it is funny.

Try to create this level of complexity in your work in the following exercises.

Deep memory Exercise:

In this exercise, we're going to work through the basics of writing a poem. This is an exercise created for the beginning poet. If you are more advanced, you might skip some of the steps or go to a more advanced exercise. If you are going to participate, read only one step at a time. Don't read ahead. You can ruin the experience by anticipating what's going to happen next.

Step one: In a quick sentence or two write down the first memory you have as a child when you were outside by yourself. Just explain it so that you understand what you're talking about. No one else is going to see this.

Step two: In an informal paragraph, write about the experience. What happened? What were you feeling? Where were you? Why do you think it sticks out in your memory as being significant?

Step three: List the following words: sight, sound, touch, taste, and smell. Next to these words, jot down all of the sights, sounds, touches, tastes, and smells you experienced.

15

Step four: Now you need to think about the dominant impression – the emotion you want to convey about that moment. Most likely, words like happiness or humor or sadness are too simplistic for the emotion that you were actually feeling. People are complex, so you don't have to write this down simply, and it doesn't have to be written for anyone else to see, so you can use personal shorthand. You might write something like: "The feeling I had at the baseball stadium that one day when I realized the coach wasn't ever going to let me play." Let your emotion be complex and even contradictory if you like.

Step five: Now that you have a sense of what your dominant impression is, go back to the words you wrote in step three. What descriptions seem to capture the emotions you were feeling? A poem doesn't have to encompass everything there, and it doesn't even have to be real. You can add description if you like that would strengthen the dominant impression.

Step six: Write the poem. We haven't started writing formal poetry yet, so you can let it be as informal as you like. You don't even need line breaks. But the point here is to write the experience as you remember it as directly as possible. Describe. Put it all into action.

You have your first draft.

Revision

Take a little time away from the poem before you do this. You're going to revise next. If the poem stirred up some emotion, don't revise until you have some emotional distance. We're practicing writing from the body in this exercise, so allow yourself to do that. If you have a good first draft and you're afraid you might lose it once you start revising, then copy the first draft, so you'll always have it.

The best way to start revising is to think about what in your poem is physical and what is merely being explained. As a poet, you want your readers not only to understand what you mean on an intellectual level, but actually to feel what you were feeling. To do that, you're going to have to focus on the descriptions and the actions in the poem.

Revision step one: Look for explanations. Are there moments when you are telling your readers what you felt or summarizing the meaning of the poem? If there are cut them out. For example, consider the following poem.

In the Imperial War Museum, February 2, 1991

The first day you found me, I was lost – off
by the gas masks and green fog of the Great
War. It was to sounds of bloody coughs
and gurgling death and all that ancient hate
that I learned love. The tour group had moved on

17

without us, but you were there to pull me
out of the wreckage of festering human
sacrifices. And you said that we
should make our break away from the cannons
of North Africa, past the rotting dead
lying in the East. You even took me from
those terrible battles raging in my head
and you brought me, my love, into the bright
London evening, just slanting towards twilight,
and that's when I fell in love with you.

This poem works pretty well until the very last
line. Beginning poets often write a poem well, they
convey the idea clearly, and then they don't trust that the
reader will understand what they've written. A great
poem with great emotional complexity is often ruined by
a line meant to summarize or explain its purpose. That
last line should be cut.

You might have several lines through your poem
that need to be cut. If it's not a direct description or an
action, consider cutting it.

Revision step two: Watch out for adjective and
adverbs. Many adjectives and adverbs that we use in
conversation are useful only in conversation. A word like
"beautiful" has meaning when spoken because the people
speaking to each other have vocal tone, a shared history,
and body language. Your reader has none of that, and the
thing is that "beautiful" means something different to
everyone.

Go through your poem looking for adjectives and
adverbs. You might keep some of them. Some of them

add to the mood or the music of the poem. However, identify each of them and cut them out if they do not.

What you're left with now is the makings of a good final draft of a poem. Rewrite the poem if you need to now keeping only those things that describe the place and your actions in the place with your dominant impression in mind.

Do the line breaks work? Try breaking it in different places to see the effect. Often short lines will increase the pacing of a poem while long lines slow it. Line breaks can do many things for a poem. If you break them mid-sentence they can create a new sort of tension or if you break them in grammatical sections, you can avoid tension. What feeling are you trying to create in the poem, and what breaks enhance that feeling?

Here are some other revision techniques you should use:

1. Read the poem out loud. We are all better listeners than readers.
2. Have a trusted friend read it to you.
3. Take a day or two away from it, and then read it again.
4. Go over it several times.

More Exercises

These exercises are for beginners and more advanced poets. I will not walk you through all the steps as I did in the first exercise, but you can always refer to those steps and use them for the new exercises. All of the following exercises are meant to create poems that come from the body. You will be creating free verse right now, but if you keep some of the ideas and images you can use these poems for your formal poetry later. Then you should compare your free verse to your formal poetry. That will give you a sense of the power and possibility of the two kinds of poetry.

Translation Exercise

This exercise is useful when you have a little writer's block. Go online and find a poem from a foreign language poet who is writing in a language you do not speak or write. Copy and paste it into Google Translator or another similar program. These programs do a good job of creating a literal translation, but your first job is going to be to try to figure out what the poet was saying and what feeling or idea s/he was trying to convey. You are going to rewrite the poem in English trying to capture the greater meaning of the original. Because of the faulty nature of the translator, what you have from the translator might not be from the body, but your job is going to be to use your skills to recreate what you think the emotion of the original was.

20

By the way, if you remain closely faithful to the original, you have just written a translation of the poem. If you stray from the original for whatever reason, you have created an original poem of your own. Either way, there's no way to fail this exercise.

Observation Exercise

Go outside to a place public, some place dynamic and interesting with a good number of people. Try to write about the place quickly, jotting down some of the key details and ideas. Get the senses down and what you see. What is it that you're feeling here? What does this place remind you of?

This is not the exercise. The reason you have traveled to some place with people is that you are not going to write this poem from your point of view. Find another person, someone who interests you. How is that person moving? What is that person doing? What does that person's emotion seem to be?

Your job now is going to be to write a persona poem. Write a poem that captures this place from that person's point of view trying to capture that person's experience and emotion.

Discomfort Exercise

This exercise can be done through memory or by creating a character. In this exercise, the narrator is out in public and feels uncomfortable for some reason. S/he might be dressed strangely or being looked at. S/he might be in a new social situation or might overhear something meant to be private.

The key is that feeling of discomfort.

The exercise is going to be to describe the discomfort in terms of the physical. What does s/he feel? Don't ever use abstract words like "discomfort" in your poem. Let us feel what s/he is feeling. Don't just report.

Chapter Two – The Power of Meter and Rhyme

Meter and rhyme are what people think of when they think of formal poetry. Meter and rhyme are often intrinsic to form. They exist to help create the music of a poem. Poetry should exist on a conscious and unconscious level for a reader. On the conscious level, readers should be able to understand the argument or point the poet is trying to make. Meter and rhyme often point these things out.

However, readers should also feel the emotions we want them to feel. Just as a drum beat creates a feeling in a song that can make the listener excited, happy, romantic, or sad, meter creates a feeling in the reader that does just about the same thing. Rhyme can do exactly the same thing to us, and there is a reason so many of us smile when we think of Dr. Seuss. How could we not? His meter and rhyme can bounce us out of serious contemplation and into good humor.

Meter

Let's start with a quick definition. Meter has to do with where we put the stresses in our words. Take for example the word "apple." "Apple" has two syllables. One of these syllables is said with more force than the other. We say "APple" rather than "apPLE." The syllable said with more force is said to be "stressed." The syllable said with less force is said to be "unstressed."

All English words have their own particular pattern of stresses and unstresses. Some words are completely unstressed. Some are completely stressed. Some have both stresses and unstresses.

This is probably not news to you, but often people wonder what the point of meter is. How could it possibly help the reading of a poem? Why would anyone bother?

Consider the following poem by Wilfred Owen:

Dulce et Decorum est

Bent double, like old beggars under sacks,
Knock-kneed, coughing like hags, we cursed through sludge,
Till on the haunting flares we turned our backs,
And towards our distant rest began to trudge.
Men marched asleep. Many had lost their boots,
But limped on, blood-shod. All went lame, all blind;
Drunk with fatigue; deaf even to the hoots
Of gas-shells dropping softly behind.

Gas! GAS! Quick, boys!—An ecstasy of fumbling
Fitting the clumsy helmets just in time,
But someone still was yelling out and stumbling
And flound'ring like a man in fire or lime.—
Dim through the misty panes and thick green light,
As under a green sea, I saw him drowning.

In all my dreams before my helpless sight
He plunges at me, guttering, choking, drowning.
If in some smothering dreams, you too could pace
Behind the wagon that we flung him in,
And watch the white eyes writhing in his face,
His hanging face, like a devil's sick of sin,
If you could hear, at every jolt, the blood

Come gargling from the froth-corrupted lungs
Bitter as the cud
Of vile, incurable sores on innocent tongues,—
My friend, you would not tell with such high zest
To children ardent for some desperate glory,
The old Lie: Dulce et decorum est
Pro patria mori.

This is a poem about World War One. The narrator of the story tells what it was like to live through the gas attacks that were so terrible they were later outlawed by the international Geneva Convention. It is broken into several sections. The meter of each section not only mirrors the emotions that exist in the poem but actually helps to create those emotions in his readers.

In the first section, Owen discusses the day-to-day pain and drudgery of long and painful marches. He recreates the tedium and pain of life in the army through the long months of fighting and moving.

Bent double, like old beggars under sacks,
Knock-kneed, coughing like hags, we cursed through sludge,
Till on the haunting flares we turned our backs,
And towards our distant rest began to trudge.
Men marched asleep. Many had lost their boots,
But limped on, blood-shod. All went lame, all blind;
Drunk with fatigue; deaf even to the hoots
Of gas-shells dropping softly behind.

The imagery in this scene helps to recreate the pain and difficulty of the soldiers, but the meter does so as well. By the time the stanza is finished, we, the readers, feel fatigued. Here, the meter is languid with most of the syllables unstressed. The meter trudges on as the soldiers are trudging on through the mud and difficulty of the war.

In the second section, however, there is a surprise gas attack on the soldiers, which the narrator learns about first from his commanding officer.

> Gas! GAS! Quick, boys!—An ecstasy of fumbling
> Fitting the clumsy helmets just in time,
> But someone still was yelling out and stumbling
> And flound'ring like a man in fire or lime.—
> Dim through the misty panes and thick green light,
> As under a green sea, I saw him drowning.
>
> In all my dreams before my helpless sight
> He plunges at me, guttering, choking, drowning.

This surprise attack is terrifying and creates an adrenaline rush in the narrator. We feel it too especially in the first four words: "Gas! GAS! Quick, boys!" which are all stressed syllables. After that the lines remain mostly stressed as the surprise and terror of the attack continues. First, the narrator is shocked. Then, he is in horror as he watches his fellow soldier writhing in pain after being poisoned by gas.

These feelings are not just explained. We actually feel the narrator's terror because of what he has done with meter.

The final section is a reflection on the experience of nearly dying and watching a poor soldier who actually drowns to death (the effect of the gas). This section is much more sedate. The narrator isn't trudging or terrified. He is reflecting on that day.

> If in some smothering dreams, you too could pace
> Behind the wagon that we flung him in,
> And watch the white eyes writhing in his face,
> His hanging face, like a devil's sick of sin,
> If you could hear, at every jolt, the blood
> Come gargling from the froth-corrupted lungs
> Bitter as the cud
> Of vile, incurable sores on innocent tongues,—
> My friend, you would not tell with such high zest
> To children ardent for some desperate glory,
> The old Lie: Dulce et decorum est
> Pro patria mori.

Here the meter is more evenly balanced between stressed and unstressed syllables. The narrator has more distance, and he wants to relate an idea that he's passionate about, but that he's not currently terrified of.

Meter can have a lot of unconscious power. While we are reading about the soldiers, we start to feel terrified and outraged ourselves. The music of the rhythm is part of what creates that feeling for us. Playing with different meters can create different feelings, and in fact, although you can set up a regular beat all the way through (many poem forms do), you can play with them as Wilfred Owen has here, and use them to create different moods throughout.

In any case, here is a list of meters. I have named them all, but it is not important for you to memorize the names necessarily. What is important is for you to try them out and see their effects.

1. Iamb   unstress, stress
2. Trochee   stress, unstress
3. Anapest   unstress, unstress, stress
4. Dactyl   stress, unstress, unstress
5. Spondee   stress, stress
6. Pyrrhic   unstress, unstress

Each one of these is called a foot. So if you have three iambic feet, you will have six syllables. If you three anapestic feet, you will have nine syllables.

Again, it is most important here is getting a sense of how these affect readers by trying them out. If you really want to get a sense of what meter can do, analyze what Lewis Carroll does in the following poem. This same poem will be used later in this book to describe the power of rhyme.

JABBERWOCKY – Lewis Carroll

'Twas brillig, and the slithy toves
Did gyre and gimble in the wabe;
All mimsy were the borogoves,
And the mome raths outgrabe.

'Beware the Jabberwock, my son!
The jaws that bite, the claws that catch!
Beware the Jubjub bird, and shun
The frumious Bandersnatch!'

He took his vorpal sword in hand:
Long time the manxome foe he sought—
So rested he by the Tumtum tree,
And stood awhile in thought.

And as in uffish thought he stood,
The Jabberwock, with eyes of flame,
Came whiffling through the tulgey wood,
And burbled as it came!

One, two! One, two! And through and through
The vorpal blade went snicker-snack!
He left it dead, and with its head
He went galumphing back.

'And hast thou slain the Jabberwock?
Come to my arms, my beamish boy!
O frabjous day! Callooh! Callay!'
He chortled in his joy.

'Twas brillig, and the slithy toves
Did gyre and gimble in the wabe;
All mimsy were the borogoves,
And the mome raths outgrabe.

Lewis Carroll shows us here what a strong sense of meter can do, especially in his first and last stanzas. It is amazing that all of the key words he uses are nonsense words, but we still have a sense that we understand what he's talking about by the end of the first stanzas. There are a number of ways that he accomplishes this effect, and one of those is his meter.

We know what we are supposed to feel throughout the poem in part because of the emotion given to us through the force of the syllables. The poem is at times reflective and at other times tense, and as the hero feels these emotions, so do we.

Scanning the Meter Exercise

This exercise might feel like the homework you did in the tenth grade. If you're more interested in getting into using meter instead of studying it, skip this part. However, a little studying can help you to understand the concept.

Part one: Look back at "Jabberwocky" and analyze the system of stress and unstresses. When, how, and why does Carroll vary what he is doing in his poetry.

Part two: Read Sir Patrick Spens

Sir Patrick Spens

The king sits in Dunfermline toune
Contented thair to dine:
"O whar will I get guid sailor,
To sail this schip of mine?"

Up and spak an eldern knicht,
Sat at the kings richt kne:
"Sir Patrick Spens is the best sailor
That sails upon the se."

The king has written a braid letter,
And signed it wi his hand,

And sent it to Sir Patrick Spens,
Was walking on the sand.

The first line that Sir Patrick red,
A loud lauch lauched he;
The next line that Sir Patrick red,
The teir blinded his ee.

"O wha is this has don this deid,
This ill deid don to me,
To send me out this time o' the yeir,
To sail upon the se!

"Mak hast, mak haste, my mirry men all,
Our guid schip sails the morne":
"O say na sae, my master deir,
For I feir a deadlie storme.

"Laie late yestreen I saw the new moone,
Wi the auld moone in her arme,
And I feir, I feir, my deir master,
That we will cum to harme."

O our Scots nobles wer richt laith
To weet their cork-heild schoone;
Bot land owre a' the play wer playd,
Thair hats they swam aboone.

O lang, lang may the ladies stand,
Wi thair gold kems in their hair,
Waiting for thair ain deir lords,
For they'll se thame na mair.

Haf owre, haf owre to Aberdour,
It's fiftie fadom deip,
And thair lies guid Sir Patrick Spens,

Wi the Scots lords at his feit.

The challenge of reading this poem is that it was written in Middle English, which is a different dialect than ours, and there were no standard spellings at that time. So the poet's "kems" is our "combs." Still you can get a sense of what he was trying to get at by analyzing the meter of the form.

Part Three: Here's one that's closer to our language. This is by William Wordsworth.

I Wandered Lonely as a Cloud

I wandered lonely as a cloud
That floats on high o'er vales and hills,
When all at once I saw a crowd,
A host, of golden daffodils;
Beside the lake, beneath the trees,
Fluttering and dancing in the breeze.

Continuous as the stars that shine
And twinkle on the milky way,
They stretched in never-ending line
Along the margin of a bay:
Ten thousand saw I at a glance,
Tossing their heads in sprightly dance.

The waves beside them danced; but they
Out-did the sparkling waves in glee:
A poet could not but be gay,
In such a jocund company:
I gazed---and gazed---but little thought
What wealth the show to me had brought:

For oft, when on my couch I lie
In vacant or in pensive mood,
They flash upon that inward eye
Which is the bliss of solitude;
And then my heart with pleasure fills,
And dances with the daffodils.

Wordsworth's poem helps to recreate the feeling of being in nature. His narrator is wandering the hills and finds joy in a field of daffodils.

Exercise of Revision

Whenever you revise a poem, there is always the danger of making it worse. Before revising anything, save the original copy, so at least if you make it worse, you have the original.

Find an old poem you wrote. If you have done exercises from this book, use one of those poems. What you are going to try to do now is change your poem based on what you've learned about meter.

It is important that you don't overwhelm yourself. So instead of thinking about changing the entire poem, take a section of it, something that has one idea. Maybe a stanza or just a section.

Ask yourself what you are trying to get at. What is the mood supposed to be? What feeling should the readers have? Revise that section with a sense of the meter.

Exercise for Feeling

Just to get a sense of how meter feels, write a line with a certain number of feet. Remember that when we're talking about a foot in poetry, we're talking about the number of syllables in an iamb, trochee, anapest, dactyl, spondee, or pyrrhic, so a foot of an anapest is three syllables and a foot of an iamb is two syllables.

For now, allow your words to be nonsense the way that Lewis Carroll did in "Jabberwocky." Try to create emotions in lines with three feet. Here are some emotions to go for:

1. Angry
2. Romantic
3. Joyful
4. Sorrowful

Rhyme

Rhyme is another musical device that can be used by writers on a very unconscious level to create feeling. It also can become memorable, but there are a number of real dangers in using it, so many good and even great free verse poets avoid it. It is perhaps the musical device most closely associated with poetry, and it's a natural part of many types of formal poetry.

Rhyme is really daunting for a lot of writers, but it becomes less scary if you remember that this is not a rule, but a tool that can help you do what you're trying to do. And what are you trying to do? You're trying to create a feeling or a mood in your poems.

And remember this. There is no pressure here. The worst thing that will happen is that you will try to rhyme and not do such a good job at it, but you'll have a poem that you crafted well using the best words you could have. There is a lot you can accomplish simply by trying to rhyme.

At its worst, a rhyme can be a distraction.

Poets can start to obsess on their need to rhyme and forget about everything else so eventually the ideas and art is lost to the need to create an exact sound. You might end up with a couplet like the following.

> "My mother has always been my favorite person.
> If you asked who is the greatest, she is the one!"

It's a nice sentiment, but a terrible couplet, and the poet knows it and becomes frustrated. First, we're going to work on learning how to avoid this kind of awkward line. Here are four concepts to think about that will help you avoid this problem.

1. Revision: rhyming well often happens when you revise. This doesn't necessarily mean getting out a whole draft of the poem before you go back and revise it. In fact, I'd probably work on revising the rhymes as you go on. Try to get down the idea first and then think about the rhyme. Don't feel

that once you have the first line down, you have to force the second line to rhyme with it. In fact, often the second line will be stronger and you should go back to change the first.

2. Enjambment versus end stop: End stop is stopping the idea at the end of the line of poetry. Most music does this. You don't have to, though. You can enjamb a line so the rhyme comes at the end of the line but in the middle of the idea. For example:

> "My mother has always been my favorite person
> to talk to. She listened and said little and was the one
> we came to when . . ."

The rhyme here is a little hidden, but it works and does so on an unconscious level. The music of the poem still exists, but it is not getting in the way of the poet.

3. Feminine v. Masculine rhymes: A masculine rhyme is one where the last syllable is stressed. A feminine rhyme has an unstressed last syllable. This makes the rhyme a little more subtle.

4. Almost rhymes: Okay, so obviously if something almost rhymes, it's not actually rhyming at all. So what? There are no rhyme police. And much of what is strong and beautiful in rhyming can be captured when you aren't actually rhyming but only coming close to rhyming. In fact, this can

often create a better mood and feeling than an actual rhyme.

The key to understanding the power of rhyming is that it's a tool that is meant to help you create something in your poetry. The moment it gets in your way, you can abandon it in part or completely. The rhyme then still has helped your poetry. Thinking about it has made you conscious of what is and is not working in your poem.

The power of the rhyme is that it helps to create music. It can do a number of things. It can work its way into a reader's subconscious, forcing him/her to feel what the poet likes or it can help to make the poem memorable. It can be overt or subtle. It can help to make the point.

Look at what it does in some of the following poems.

We looked at "Jabberwocky" in the "Meter" section of this chapter. At that time, I talked about how meter helps to create meaning and feeling. Even through many of these words are nonsense, we still understand the poem on a very basic and emotional level. When the poem is dreamy and idyllic, so is the rhythm. When it is heroic, the rhythm is too.

It works in this same way on the level of rhyme. The rhymes in this poem help to reflect the emotion of the characters and the narrator. When there is tension, we feel it.

Jabberwocky – Lewis Carroll

'Twas brillig, and the slithy toves
Did gyre and gimble in the wabe;
All mimsy were the borogoves,
And the mome raths outgrabe.

'Beware the Jabberwock, my son!
The jaws that bite, the claws that catch!
Beware the Jubjub bird, and shun
The frumious Bandersnatch!'

He took his vorpal sword in hand:
Long time the manxome foe he sought—
So rested he by the Tumtum tree,
And stood awhile in thought.

And as in uffish thought he stood,
The Jabberwock, with eyes of flame,
Came whiffling through the tulgey wood,
And burbled as it came!

One, two! One, two! And through and through
The vorpal blade went snicker-snack!
He left it dead, and with its head
He went galumphing back.

'And hast thou slain the Jabberwock?
Come to my arms, my beamish boy!
O frabjous day! Callooh! Callay!'
He chortled in his joy.

'Twas brillig, and the slithy toves
Did gyre and gimble in the wabe;
All mimsy were the borogoves,
And the mome raths outgrabe.

Sound works on a deeply psychological level for human beings. There is a reason skunks are called "skunks." There is something as profoundly disagreeable about the sound as there is about being near the animal, and it is no coincidence that "cactus" is such a cacophonous sound. It is also not a coincidence that most of us don't use the word "pulchritudinous." It sounds terrible even though it means "beautiful."

Most of us have some degree of synesthesia, a psychological and physical condition where two or more senses become confused. It does not make sense that there could be sharp sounds and soft sounds, but most of us understand what it means to have a sharp sound.

This is a strange aspect of the human mind, that we confuse the senses so often. I suppose it puts us in a surreal kind of existence, but it is a wise poet who understands that the pleasure of poetry goes beyond the logical and into the deeply weird places in our brains.

Lewis Carroll knew that, and his understanding of how weird we truly are made his surrealist poetry beautiful and meaningful. You don't have to go as far as he did, but understanding what he did will help you to create something meaningful in your own work.

"Jabberwocky" Exercise:

To give yourself a sense of exactly what rhyme can accomplish, this exercise will have you run through a number of drills where you are using nonsense words.

The hope is that you get a sense of just how sounds even without meaning can affect the reading of a poem. It's important though that you read your work out loud when you're done so you are able to get a sense of what you have accomplished.

Part One: Write a heroic couplet using nonsense words. A heroic couplet has two lines that rhyme with each other at the end. It should have five iambic feet (see the "Meter" section of this chapter). Not all of your words need to be completely meaningless, but the key words, especially those that rhyme, should be. Rewrite that rhyme using a sharp sound, soft sound, masculine rhyme, and feminine rhyme.

Part Two: Write four lines of poetry using nonsense words. The second line should rhyme with the fourth line. Again, not every word needs to be nonsense, just the key words. Revise it using both sharp and soft sounds.

Part Three: Write four lines of poetry using nonsense words. The first and third lines should rhyme, and these lines should be enjambed. Rewrite that rhyme using a sharp sound, soft sound, masculine rhyme, and feminine rhyme.

The Translation Exercise Redux

Earlier in this book, there was an exercise that had you find a foreign language poem and translated it into English using Google Translator or a similar program. You were to translate the poem into English but to keep the feeling of the original. This exercise asks you to do the same thing.

You do not, however, need to translate the entire poem. This is an exercise meant to give you a sense of what rhyme can do. If you like, try translating just a section or just a stanza.

You will need to start by figuring out what the poet was trying to say. Chances are that the original will not translate well into English. There is only so much we could expect from a translation program, after all.

After you have a sense of what the poet was going for, you need to decide what kind of rhyme scheme you want. Is the poem heroic or elegiac? Is it meant to excite us or put us in a contemplative point of view? Is it supposed to be funny?

All of these questions and more should affect your rhyme scheme. You are going to need to choose the correct rhyme scheme for the emotion you're getting at.

The In-Remembrance Exercise

Start this exercise by going into your memory. Consider a place you once knew well and the way you felt when you were there. This does not have to be a place that you liked. In fact, you might get a much better poem if it's some place that you didn't like.

You're going to write about this place.

Part One: What did you feel when you were there? Most emotions are more complex than a single word. Use some kind of shorthand that you understand. No one is going to see this but you.

Part Two: What were the physical sensations of being there?

Part Three: Write your poem. As much as possible, just try to capture the physical sensation of being there, and trust that your readers are going to understand the point of what you're getting at. Do not write any lines meant to summarize or explain the experience. Your readers are smart. After all, they're reading your work.

You're going to have to figure out what lines to rhyme and why you rhyme those lines. Exactly what effect are you going for here? For this poem, consider enjambing most of the lines to create a subtlety to your poetry that works on a subconscious level.

Also remember that there is no such thing as failure in this project. If some of your lines don't rhyme exactly perfectly, well that's all right. You have an unrhymed poem where every word is carefully considered. People have written much worse poetry.

The Bizarre Rhyme Scheme Poem

Rhyme doesn't have to be exact to have an effect on us. When you get to the sestina, you'll be given a completely new way to think of rhyme and line endings.

In this exercise, you're going to play with rhyme quite a bit.

Your poem is going to be broken into two stanzas. Each stanza will be eight lines. The first stanza you should approach as if it were a free verse poem. Just write it, trying to capture a moment in time.

In the second stanza, every line should rhyme with a line in the first stanza. However, you don't need to have any regularity at all. For example, the first line of stanza two could rhyme with the sixth line of stanza one. The fourth and eighth lines could rhyme with stanza one's second line.

The careful consideration of each line and what you're doing with it should be the most important element that comes through the poem.

Chapter Three – The Sonnet

When people think of formal poetry they most often think of the sonnet. It is the poem type that most people are familiar with because in high school, it is the form that we are forced to read most often.

Because so much of the old poetry we read is in the sonnet form, sonnets are both familiar and scary. After all, Keats wrote sonnets. Wordsworth wrote sonnets. Gasp, Shakespeare wrote sonnets. It's hard to live up to that kind of poetic weight, but the thing is that you don't have to do that. You don't have to live up to anything.

The sonnet is not a form with rules and a tradition that you have to live up to; the sonnet is a form with tools that can help you.

You might have to change your mind set a little. Writing in form is different than writing free verse. Generally, when you're writing free verse you have a good idea of what you want to say, and you create a form that helps you to express that idea.

When you write in form, you need to let go. You might not have any idea of what you're going to write, and just let the form create the poem. Alternatively, you might have some kind of idea and let the form guide you through the poem.

The sonnet has a very strong structure, so each line of the poem suggests the next line and even the line before it. Once you understand that, you do not have to worry about anything except working on the line you are on. If you capture clear imagery and follow the conventions of the form. That will be enough to create a strong poem.

There are different kinds of sonnets, but the two most common kinds are the Petrarchan Sonnet and the Shakespearian Sonnet. Both sonnet types are fourteen lines long, use iambic pentameter (that is, they have five iambic feet), and have a specific rhyme scheme. The difference between these two sonnet forms is in their rhyme scheme and the way they build to a point.

Before you start writing a modern sonnet, we'll go over some older sonnets to give you a sense of the basic form. Don't worry if you become overwhelmed by this discussion. Just read through it and how you can use it to your advantage will be explained later.

The Petrarchan Sonnet

On His Blindness – John Milton

When I consider how my light is spent (a)
Ere half my days, in this dark world and wide, (b)
And that one talent which is death to hide, (b)
Lodged with me useless, though my soul more bent (a)
To serve therewith my Maker, and present (a)
My true account, lest he returning chide; (b)
"Doth God exact day-labor, light denied?" (b)
I fondly ask; but Patience to prevent (a)
That murmur, soon replies, "God doth not need (c)
Either man's work or his own gifts; who best (d)
Bear his mild yoke, they serve him best. His state (e)

Is Kingly. Thousands at his bidding speed (c)
And post o'er land and ocean without rest; (d)
They also serve who only stand and wait." (e)

The Petrarchan Sonnet is broken into three general sections. There are two sections of four lines each.

When I consider how my light is spent (a)
Ere half my days, in this dark world and wide, (b)
And that one talent which is death to hide, (b)
Lodged with me useless, though my soul more bent (a)

To serve therewith my Maker, and present (a)
My true account, lest he returning chide; (b)
"Doth God exact day-labor, light denied?" (b)
I fondly ask; but Patience to prevent (a)

Notice the rhyme scheme. The first line rhymes with the fourth, fifth, and eighth. The second line rhymes with the third, sixth, and seventh. Here, Milton's narrator mourns the loss of his eye sight, and he wonders how God expects for Milton to serve Him with his blindness.

That murmur, soon replies, "God doth not need (c)
Either man's work or his own gifts; who best (d)
Bear his mild yoke, they serve him best. His state (e)
Is Kingly. Thousands at his bidding speed (c)
And post o'er land and ocean without rest; (d)
They also serve who only stand and wait." (e)

The rhyme scheme in the last six lines can vary. In this poem, it is cdecde, but it can also be cdccdc or cdcdcd.

In the first two sections, the poet should propose a problem. The last section should solve that problem. Here Milton's narrator hears the voice of "Patience" telling him that all he need to do is to wait patiently for God's will.

The Shakespearean Sonnet

Sonnet 130 – Shakespeare

My mistress' eyes are nothing like the sun; (a)
Coral is far more red than her lips' red; (b)
If snow be white, why then her breasts are dun; (a)
If hairs be wires, black wires grow on her head. (b)
I have seen roses damasked, red and white, (c)
But no such roses see I in her cheeks; (d)
And in some perfumes is there more delight(c)
Than in the breath that from my mistress reeks. (d)
I love to hear her speak, yet well I know (e)
That music hath a far more pleasing sound; (f)
I grant I never saw a goddess go; (e)
My mistress when she walks treads on the ground. (f)
    And yet, by heaven, I think my love as rare (g)
    As any she belied with false compare. (g)

The rhyme scheme of the Shakespearean sonnet often makes the rhymes more apparent to the reader of the Shakespearean Sonnet. It's broken into four parts.

Sonnet 130 – Shakespeare

My mistress' eyes are nothing like the sun; (a)
Coral is far more red than her lips' red; (b)
If snow be white, why then her breasts are dun; (a)
If hairs be wires, black wires grow on her head. (b)

47

I have seen roses damasked, red and white, (c)
But no such roses see I in her cheeks; (d)
And in some perfumes is there more delight(c)
Than in the breath that from my mistress reeks. (d)

The first two parts set up a situation or problem and create an internal rhyme scheme. In this case, Shakespeare compares his mistress (meaning his girlfriend, wife, or lover, not necessarily what we think of as a mistress) to objects in nature, and says that she is not as beautiful as these things. Her eyes are less beautiful than the sun. Here lips are dull compared to coral, and so on.

I love to hear her speak, yet well I know (e)
That music hath a far more pleasing sound; (f)
I grant I never saw a goddess go; (e)
My mistress when she walks treads on the ground. (f)

The third section can either continue this problem or situation or start to solve it. In this case, Shakespeare continues to say that his mistress is not nearly as beautiful as natural things. Your poem can start to suggest a solution or a change here if you like.

And yet, by heaven, I think my love as rare (g)
As any she belied with false compare. (g)

The last two lines either summarize the situation, or, if it is a problem, suggest a surprising twist or solution. Shakespeare writes that even though he refuses to lie about his mistress's beauty, he still loves her completely, and in fact, one might infer that he loves her more than most people who lie. He loves the real woman. He doesn't just lust after her body.

These are the basics of sonnet writing, and they seem fairly daunting, but we're going to build towards making the process easy.

Here are some more modern sonnets written by Donna Hilbert:

Traveler

You come at night to say you're leaving,
have dreamed of freedom for so long.
And more, you love another—old familiar song.
I call for Mother in my grieving,
but in her own dream, she's not speaking.
The children, uninvolved, won't say you're wrong.
Our friends are not surprised, say don't prolong
the misery, the pain, by not accepting
that you're gone. Because I refuse to hear
the first time you say you really have to go,
you speak again, louder than before, and wear
a new love on your arm, gesture meant to show
you have no love for me—I must forbear.
The dead are even colder than we know.

Peninsula, Long Beach

On this beach the days are mild, evenings cool.
Wind kicks up at three, unvaried as bread
sliced from a single loaf. I read
the seasons by the setting sun: summer's spool
hidden by high rise, and then, the slow pull
toward Catalina. By fall, the sun beds
down in open ocean, un-obscured
except by cruise and cargo ships schooled
before the port. Neighbors say Upton Sinclair
left Pasadena to summer on this beach.
I wonder how he conjured slaughter
houses—the severed flesh, the stench—in air
so sweet? Did suffering stay within his reach
while dolphins leapt and sun melted to water?

Here's one by Caroline Gill:

Cornish Evening

The sun dips down and hides beneath the waves
as storm clouds gather in the western sky.
A seagull hovers round the empty caves:
I heed the warning of its hue and cry.

The stackhouse stands to guard the ancient mine:
a hidden path leads down towards the bay
where Cornish smugglers waded through the brine
to stash their stores of contraband away.

A lightship shoots its beam across the sea:
the old cliff castle stands serene and still.
But wait, within its walls there seems to be
a small parade assembling on the hill.

I strain to see the shadows through the night:
no soldiers these – their tails are round and white.

For Beginning Poets

There are a number of different aspects to the sonnet. We're going to create a new kind of sonnet for the first exercise called the unrhymed and unmetered sonnet. In this sonnet, you don't have to rhyme or have meter. You just need to have fourteen lines with ten syllables per line. In the first eight lines, you need to set up a problem or a situation. In the last six lines, you need to suggest a solution or a new way of looking at the situation.

For this poem, start off with moment when you felt awkward. Remember to write from the body and let us know what it was like to feel that way. When you get to the last six lines, explain why this feeling of anxiety was misplaced or wrong.

At this point, you should not worry about the meter or rhyme. You're just seeing what is possible in fourteen lines with ten syllables per line.

For More Advanced Poets – The Line Replacement Method

The fact is that many of the great poets have written sonnets, so we have thousands of good sonnets. You don't want to plagiarize anyone, but taking a great poet's rhymes isn't plagiarizing. Read the following poem:

Written in London, September 1802 –William Wordsworth

> O Friend! I know not which way I must look
> For comfort, being, as I am, opprest,
> To think that now our life is only drest
> For show; mean handy-work of craftsman, cook,
> Or groom! — We must run glittering like a brook
> In the open sunshine, or we are unblest:
> The wealthiest man among us is the best:
> No grandeur now in nature or in book
> Delights us. Rapine, avarice, expense,
> This is idolatry; and these we adore:
> Plain living and high thinking are no more:
> The homely beauty of the good old cause
> Is gone; our peace, our fearful innocence,
> And pure religion breathing household laws.

This poem had great relevance in Wordsworth's time. The problems that he was dealing with were serious to his mind and reality. The problems that we deal with are just as serious to us. You're going to update this poem to be relevant to your life. In the end, you will be left only with his rhyming words and perhaps even they will change.

Start by changing "opprest" to "oppressed," "drest" to "dressed," and "unblest" to "unblessed." The spellings that he used are antiquated. You might argue that this makes "best" a near rhyme, and you'd be right; however, near rhymes are all right.

Take the following line out of the middle of the poem, "No grandeur now in nature or in book." This line is going to stay in the middle of the poem, but you're going to work with it first.

Don't think about the rest of the poem. Simply try to write a line that ends with the word "book." It can even be enjambed. Here's mine: "When I looked over at my friend's MacBook,"

This is not a perfect line. It doesn't need to me. It's a draft. Now the poem which is mostly Wordsworth but in part is mine reads:

> O Friend! I know not which way I must look
> For comfort, being, as I am, oppressed,
> To think that now our life is only dressed
> For show; mean handy-work of craftsman, cook,
> Or groom! — We must run glittering like a brook
> In the open sunshine, or we are unblessed:
> The wealthiest man among us is the best:
> When I looked over at my friend's MacBook,
> Delights us. Rapine, avarice, expense,
> This is idolatry; and these we adore:
> Plain living and high thinking are no more:
> The homely beauty of the good old cause
> Is gone; our peace, our fearful innocence,
> And pure religion breathing household laws.

The poem doesn't make sense any longer, but the good thing is all I really have to do is concentrate on one line. I only have to finish the next sentence, and all I have to do at this moment is explain what happens when the narrator looks at the MacBook described in the poem,

keeping in mind that my last word needs to be "expense."
My two lines will read:

> When I looked over at my friend's MacBook,
> he had joked on a thread at the expense

Now the poem seems to be going in an interesting direction. I think if I continue it, it will turn into a story that has something to do with the idea of cyber-bullying. I didn't have any idea that I was going to discuss cyber-bullying before I started. The sonnet form just pulled it out of me. Once I changed that first line and changed "book" to "MacBook" the form pulled the idea out of me.

I have two choices now: to finish this sentence by going on to the next line or to try to go back to the line before and figure out what would have come before this.

Soon enough, you're going to have a sonnet that works. If one of the end words doesn't fit in, change it. But for the most part, try to keep the same words.

By concentrating on simply writing line by line, and replacing words, you are going to end up with a strong poem.

And the truth is that since each line suggests the next, you can start by simply replacing one word. Once that word has been changed, it will suggest the next word, and the next, and the next.

Your poem is almost certainly going to be missing a few things. Probably the meter won't be exact. My two lines certainly are not iambic. Remember that this is just an exercise getting you ready to write your own sonnet. However, you should also remember that you can always use Wordsworth's or Shakespeare's rhymes or anyone else's for that matter.

You will almost certainly not have followed the pattern of having a turn for the last six lines. That's all right too. So now what you have is something that's pretty close to being a perfect sonnet.

For Very Advanced Poets

Take Wordsworth's poem from the last exercise and simply keep the rhymes. Write your own poem based on these. Focus line by line. When you come to the end of the eighth line, you need to stop. Ask yourself at this point what argument you have made. What is the situation or the problem? How can the last six lines offer a solution? Focus line by line. Work on writing from the body. The themes and meanings will push themselves out. You do not need to work on that. You simply need to focus on creating.

More Exercises:

A Second Exercise for the Line Replacement Method:

Just as you did earlier, work on the following poem, replacing a middle line but keeping as many of the rhyming words as possible. This time break it into two sections. Think of these sections as two poems. In the first section, you will propose or even just illustrate a problem. In the second section, you will solve that problem.

Sonnet 25 – William Shakespeare

Let those who are in favour with their stars
Of public honour and proud titles boast,
Whilst I, whom fortune of such triumph bars
Unlook'd for joy in that I honour most.
Great princes' favourites their fair leaves spread
But as the marigold at the sun's eye,
And in themselves their pride lies buried,
For at a frown they in their glory die.
The painful warrior famoused for fight,
After a thousand victories once foiled,
Is from the book of honour razed quite,
And all the rest forgot for which he toiled:
      Then happy I, that love and am beloved,
      Where I may not remove nor be removed.

Further Reading

Tony Barnstone's "Manifesto on the Contemporary Sonnet" is an excellent discussion of how the sonnet form can be used by current writers. This is mandatory reading for anyone who wants to truly master the form. It can be found online on several different websites.

On Your Blindness Exercise

In John Milton's "On His Blindness," Milton discusses a problem that he absolutely cannot change.

He's blind. In his frustration, he tries to find meaning in his life since his work as a poet demands his eyesight.

Part One: What is a problem that you feel powerless to change? This might be anything from a physical problem, to an emotional problem, to a situational problem.

Part Two: Write the first eight lines of a Petrarchan Sonnet outlining that problem.

Part Three: Milton cannot really solve his problem. He realizes that all he can really do is view the purpose of his life in a different way than he did in the past. He decides to be patient.
        Try to view your own problem this way. If there is no solution, what can you do? What should you do?

Part Four: Write the last six lines of the sonnet discussing this new mindset.

The "This Is Growing Up" Exercise

As we grow older, we understand places and people in a completely different way. The sonnet is a great form for showing how our understanding of the world changes and evolves. The first eight lines of this exercise will be an exploration of how you understood someone you loved when you were younger. In the second six lines, you will change to an older perspective and show how your understanding of that person changed when you had grown up.

Chapter Four – The Villanelle

There is a musicality to the villanelle that makes the form memorable and at times powerful and other times charming. Some of our most beloved poems are villanelles because the rhyme and repetition builds and sustains poetic tension and helps us to remember the poem and brings home the poet's your point.

But what is a villanelle?

A villanelle is a relatively young form of poetry with a very specific structure. A villanelle must have:

1. Nineteen lines.
2. These lines are broken in to six stanzas. The first five stanzas have three lines each. The final stanza has four lines.
3. There are only two rhymes.
4. The first line is repeated as the sixth, twelfth, and eighteenth lines.
5. The third line is repeated as the ninth, fifth, and nineteenth lines.
6. There are no rules for the meter.

The poetic scheme looks like this:

Line 1 (A)
Line 2 (B)
Line 3 (A)

Line 4 (A)
Line 5 (B)

Line 6 (A) Repeats Line 1

Line 7 (A)
Line 8 (B)
Line 9 (A) Repeats Line 2

Line 10 (A)
Line 11 (B)
Line 12 (A) Repeats Line 1

Line 13 (A)
Line 14 (B)
Line 15 (A) Repeats Line 2

Line 16 (A)
Line 17 (B)
Line 18 (A) Repeats Line 1
Line 19 (A) Repeats Line 2

This all looks very complicated when it is described abstractly. However, the result is often amazing. Dylan Thomas's "Do Not Go Gentle into that Good Night" and Elizabeth Bishop's "One Art" (both can be found on several sites online) are examples of truly brilliant poems. Bishop's poem also is a fine example of how playing with the form and changing the lines that repeat in subtle ways can create greater meaning. Here's another strong example by Edward Arlington Robinson:

The House on the Hill

They are all gone away,
The House is shut and still,
There is nothing more to say.

Through broken walls and gray
The winds blow bleak and shrill.
They are all gone away.

Nor is there one to-day
To speak them good or ill:
There is nothing more to say.

Why is it then we stray
Around the sunken sill?
They are all gone away,

And our poor fancy-play
For them is wasted skill:
There is nothing more to say.

There is ruin and decay
In the House on the Hill:
They are all gone away,
There is nothing more to say.

Here is a more modern villanelle by Donna
Hilbert:

To Make a Salad

Choose your lettuce wisely, wash it well
and store in plastic sealed with a cushion of air.
The leafy greens that local growers sell

stay fresh a week on top refrigerator shelves.
So, move the milk and keep your greenery there.
Choose your produce wisely, store it well.

Use arugula, spinach, red chard, fennel
to lend your salads variety and flair.
Pick seasoning herbs organic grocers sell.

Pinch dill, mint, basil to release the smell
of Southern France—a heady treat to prepare
salad greens picked wisely and dressed well

in vinegar and oil. What better than a salad to tell
the season's story? Add some nuts, perhaps a pear
and cheese to the greens that local growers sell.

Food is meant for pleasure, not just to quell
the hunger pain. Cooking is an act of self-repair.
Choose fellow diners wisely, feed them well
from the plural bounty local growers sell.

There are a number of elements that need to be
discussed to understand how this poem form can be used.

The Rhyme

There danger here is that the two rhymes come
around so often that the poem can become sing-songy.
However, that opens up both dangers and possibilities.
The danger is that your poem can become silly. The
possibility is that it can be beautifully musical.

If you want to downplay the rhyme, you can do
that in two ways. First, you can enjamb some or all of the

lines. Robinson enjambs several of his lines. For example, his tenth and eleventh line read:

> Why is it then we stray
> Around the sunken sill?

This way the punctuation does not emphasize the rhyme. The rhyme becomes buried in the sentence. Of course, you might want to have the rhyme emphasized as he does in his first stanza:

> They are all gone away,
> The House is shut and still,
> There is nothing more to say.

This stanza has a heavy end stop. The effect is that we hear the rhymes more clearly. Our attention is directed towards the rhyme creating a memorable effect.

What Robinson also could have done to de-emphasize the impact of the rhyme would have been to vary the line lengths. His lines usually have six or seven syllables, but there is no reason for him to have lines that have as few as one syllable and as many syllables as he likes.

As long as the poem moves and is capturing the effect that he wants it to capture, the form of the villanelle is working.

The Meter

There is no meter that you have to follow when writing a villanelle. However, since the form is naturally musical, playing with different meters can have surprising effects. For example, using dactyls as your feet could create a poem that feels like a waltz whereas using no set rhythm would give you some of the benefits of free verse, such as having the ability to vary the mood from section to section, and some of the benefits of form, such as having the repetition of the first and third lines.

The key here is to play with the form a bit to see what it can do.

The Repeated Lines

In general, the repeated lines can do two things for you.

First, they can help to emphasize the overall point of the poem. In Dylan Thomas's "Do Not Go Gentle into that Good Night," the narrator is arguing with his father, telling him that he should not give up and die easily. Both repeated lines, "Do not go gentle into that good night" and "Rage, rage against the dying of the light" repeat the same idea. He wants to emphasize the fact that people should not give up at the end of their lives but continue to fight against death. This repetition helps that idea.

Second, they can indicate a growing understanding of a greater truth. The repeated line can gain meaning throughout the poem so that by the end of the poem, we have a greater understanding and respect for the topic. Elizabeth Bishop's "One Art" has exactly this effect. As she repeats line "The art of losing isn't hard to master," we gain an understanding of what she means by "loss." She starts by losing her keys, and ends by losing cities and people she loves, but in the end realizes that it's no disaster really to lose anything. She also changes the lines when she feels like it so they have slightly different meaning.

That's all right. Bishop's poem is a masterpiece, and there are no villanelle police to tell her to change her lines.

You should also consider the structure of those lines. Elizabeth Bishop changed her lines to build meanings. However, if you start with a word that can be used as different parts of speech depending on the situation, or if you start with a verb, so your line could be a command or the verb phrase supporting the subject of the sentence, then you will have some flexibility.

You might even consider using only half sentences for your repeated line. The first line would be the half of the sentence while the third line is the second half of the sentence. When they come together in the end, they will form a complete sentence. Until then, they will give you a good deal of flexibility in meaning and execution. I have done this in the Near-anelle below.

The Art of the Villanelle Isn't Hard to Master

Like the sonnet, the villanelle can draw ideas out of you that you never knew you had. If you trust the form, you can start letting the form work for you to help you create a poem.

The next few exercises are designed to get you to the place where you can create a villanelle, even if what you're doing at first isn't strictly a villanelle itself.

The Near-anelle

To get a sense of what the repetition can do for you, you're going to write a poem that follows all of the rules of the villanelle except that it does not rhyme. Here's an example:

I Know This Much

10 million burn silently by themselves tonight. I know
them from the roads and the silent rides home. I know them
      at least
this much. Do they go home only to sleep together alone?

I've spent my days next to them, spying on them out
my window, waiting for the blaring quiet to end, but on the
      freeway
10 million burn silently by themselves tonight. I know

what's in their head -- the thoughts of home, love, and the
      promise
of some green future, and the idea that they can take no more
      than

this much. Do they go home only to sleep together alone?

I've spent my life wanting to touch them, wondering what it
        would be
to sit in their cars with them, and if they would talk to me, but
10 million burn silently by themselves tonight. I know

it's the 10 million that does it, and the thought of the one
and how good it could be, and how they never even wanted
this much. Do they go home only to sleep together alone?

And I know what it is to sit among them, hating them and
        loving
them and wondering if anyone has ever lived any other way.
10 million burn silently by themselves tonight. I know
this much. Do they go home only to sleep together alone?

The repetition works like a refrain and is still musical and the fact that it repeats so often creates an almost manic worry about the subject.

For your Near-anelle, you're going to want to develop your repeated lines first. Think about something in your world that disturbs you. At the time I wrote the poem above, I was commuting four hours a day through Los Angeles traffic, feeling very lonely and feeling as though I was surrounded by lonely people on the freeway.

The repetition can heighten the sense that you are being bothered by some idea or problem. So your first though should be what bothers you? Develop that into your repeated lines.

After you have developed your Near-anelle, you are ready for a villanelle.

67

The Line Theft Exercise

You are going to allow the form of the villanelle and fate decide what your first real villanelle is going to be. For this exercise, you are going to read a newspaper, either online or in print. The first repeated of your villanelle is going to be the headline of the most interesting story you see.

Newspapers put a lot of time and effort into the titles of their articles. They usually end up with something interesting and poetic. You can use it, and if you put it in quotation marks, you're not really stealing it.

Now, construct your poem around that story.
Ask yourself:
1. Why is this story interesting?
2. What are the details that make it interesting?
3. Who are the key people?
4. What have they done?
5. What lesson should people learn from what has happened? (This should form the basis of the second repeated line).

Develop your villanelle with these concepts in mind, but don't allow the themes to control the poem. The only way to get something here that is of value is to concentrate on the individual lines in the moment. Trust that you will have something of value when you are finished. If you worry about the greater ideas of theme, you will end up with something weak.

Another way to say this is that you should write from the body. If you focus on the physical, everything else will just fall into place.

The Google Theft Exercise

The Google Theft Exercise is related to and builds on The Line Theft Exercise. There was a reason that you chose the news article that you chose for the last exercise. In this exercise, you are going to build on that idea.

Find a good search engine like Google and start randomly searching using keywords from the article in the last exercise. There is a lot of wackiness on the web and some profundity too. You are going to inevitably run into an article or a quotation that is going to look at the same concept in the article from a completely new way. You are now going to write a companion piece to your last villanelle, now coming to the event or concept from this completely different point of view.

Here is another example of a villanelle by Caroline Gill:

Arnside: Waiting for the Bore

I sit where silver sands stretch far away,
and wait for rising waves to rush again.
I watch the waking world, and wonder why

the ranks of wading wildfowl like to stray
in brackish pools, where sunlit shadows shine:

I sit where silver sands stretch far away.

Why does the woodland whitethroat seem so shy?
It darts like lightning through the celandine.
I watch the waking world, and wonder why

those surging summer tides turn to obey
the lunar laws, that sky and sea ordain.
I sit where silver sands stretch far away,

while sweeping siren-swifts, in blue and grey,
waft through the Arnside air and then are gone.
I watch the waking world and wonder why,

like rustling warblers in the ripened rye,
the tidal roll of roaring wave began.
I sit where silver sands stretch far away:
I watch the waking world, and wonder why.

Chapter Five – The Sestina

The sestina has no rules for meter, and there is no real rhyme necessary. Instead, the last word of every line will be repeated in a very specific pattern. The result is a poem that builds a single concept in a very musical way. It is longer than the sonnet or the villanelle, so the poet is able to build on concepts more fully here than in other poem forms, and because the line lengths tend to vary, there is a free verse feeling to it.

The basics of the sestina are that it must have 39 lines with seven stanzas. The first six stanzas are six lines long each. The last stanza is 3 lines long. The last word of every line in the first stanza will be repeated as the last words of every other stanza but in different orders (see below). In the last stanza, two of the end words are in each line.

The key to the sestina is finding the perfect words to end your lines. You need words that have significant meaning but also multiple connotations. To make things easier, you probably will want to use one or two words that are common such as "is" or "I." This is not necessary, but some people find the form easier if there is a word or two that is a little easier to use.

Here is the form. The numbers correspond to the last word of the stanza.

Stanza One

1

2

3

4

5

6

Stanza Two

6

1

5

2

4

3

Stanza Three

3

6

4

1

2

5

Stanza Four

5

3

2

6

1

4

Stanza Five
4
5
1
3
6
2

Stanza Six
2
4
6
5
3
1

Stanza Seven
2 – 5
4 – 3
6 – 1

Here is an example of the form by the poet Lloyd Aquino:

Illusions

It's only a magic trick.
Notice how the light
fixtures burst into sharp birds every time

he's about to transmogrify, molting his skin
to red curtains while he plays dead.
It's all sleight of hand.

A roomful of hushes slide off hand-
sanitized inch-thick glass. The trick
is making the audience believe he is dead
wrong, that the chains are not light
around bone-infested arms, all the skin
compressed to thinnest air, and there's no time

left to escape the shark-infested tank. This time,
it won't matter what his sly off hand
tries. There are more than a dozen ways to skin
a man, starting at the elbows, turning this trick
into phantasmagoria, all that light
crumpling to shadow monsters. Drowning in applause, he lies
dead.

But don't be fooled. When it's dead
quiet, the stage swallows what's left of the prestige. Time
for the man behind the magician to find the light,
sloughing black jacket that hangs off each hand,
claws at his back for dear life, then drops, no trick
to it at all, his clothes empty of everything but skin

and sweat. Translucent skin
with filament veins. Dead
skin to mingle with the stage dust. He can't trick
you now that you know when to fog the mirrors and how to
time
eyeblinks to his misdirection. He could hand
you a card, instruct you hold it up to the light,

but he couldn't read your mind, your spotlight
glare blinding him senseless, all that milky skin

layer-caking his eyes. Here's all it takes to cut a man in half: a hand
saw sharp as dead
and a little time.
It's what to do with the remains is the trick.

Blindfold the man and light him a cigarette to combust to. Hand
him the still-beating heart up his sleeve. Trick him out of his livery and let his skin
tell you secrets. Make sure he stays dead this time.

Notice that the end word of the sixth line in each stanza is the end word of the first line in the next stanza. There is an elegance to the way that these words repeat, and the structure of the lines help to create a feeling that is often mourning, as though the poet has an idea that he simply cannot let go and keeps coming back to.

Here are some possible dangers however:

1. If you are not writing from the body, that is writing images and sensations, your sestina will tend to go nowhere because there is no way to build meaning as you go through the poem. Abstract terms tend to kill your poems, and this problem is more dangerous in the sestina because the abstract terms will be repeated.

2. You need to have versatile words as your end words. If you do not, it is also difficult to build meanings. If you word has only one

denotation and very little connotation, then there is no way to build.

3. You need to also avoid having too many common words or the power and musicality of the sestina will be defeated. If all of your end words are common words, then the fact that they are repeated will be lost.

In general, a good strategy as a beginner is to find some key words and some common words, so you have the musicality of the form, but you are not bound to these key words in every line.

Two Ways of Approaching the Sestina

There are two basic ways of approaching the sestina. The first is to develop a first stanza about a concept that you are interested in and developing that concept from there, sticking with the key words. The second is to come up with the end words, and allowing the form to create your poem for you. In both cases after the first stanza the form of the sestina will guide your ideas, but with the first approach, you will have a general idea about what you're going to discuss in the poem.

The First Approach – Writing What You Know that You Know

Often, poets will have a good line or good couple of lines from bad poems or poems that just go nowhere.

If you have some of those, the sestina might work really well for you. You also might have a good idea, but you're not sure what to do with it. Again, the sestina will help you work that idea out. Even if you don't end up with a good sestina, one of the gifts of the sestina is that it will help you to work out your ideas.

When you approach this method for developing your sestina, start with a six line stanza. You are not going to need to have any particular structure or form, just make sure that your lines are strong and based on the physical. The challenge is going to be to know where to break your lines because, of course, these end words are going to be all important.

It's time to break out those ideas and lines that you love but don't know how to use. The sestina exists to show you how to use them.

If you don't have those lines, and you want to work with this, think about something in your life that you regret. The sestina is an excellent form for poems of lament, mourning, and dissatisfaction because the music that it creates is often so obsessive and repetitive. Each successive stanza almost naturally dwells on the same concept but looking at it from a new perspective.

The Second Approach – Writing What You Didn't Know You Knew

If you have the ability to write formal poetry, there should never be a moment when you experience writer's block. If you are stuck for an idea, you can always fall back on a form and allow that form to give you the ideas you didn't realize were inside of you.

The sestina does this better than any other form.

The key is finding the six words that will form the end of your lines. If you have the right six words, you will have the basis of a poem, and each of those words will give you ideas. You want a mixture of key words and common words, so you have the music of the poem, but you are not forced to constantly say the same thing in each stanza.

The question is, how do you find them? Here are a few methods for finding your end words.

1. End word plagiarism: This isn't actually plagiarism. Use the end words from a different sestina. You aren't going to write the same things as the original poet because you have different sensibilities and a different life experience.
2. Google fun: Go on random Google searches until the words pop out at you.
3. Favorites search: What's your favorite poem or novel? Chances are part of the reason you love that is the language the author or poet uses. Steal some of that writer's words.
4. Word of the day: There are any number of websites that have Word of the Day functions. Construct a poem out of an interesting word of the day.

Probably the best way to do this is to think about a general theme you're interested in. A few years ago, my house was nearly burned down in a forest fire. I think about that time in my life every so often, and I think I could develop a good poem about it. I'm not sure what I would say, but here are the end words I might use:

1. Fire (This a key word that can be used as a noun, verb, and even an adjective. It can also be used metaphorically or literally. The danger with this word is falling into cliché, however.)
2. Forest (This is another key word. It is an evocative word and physical. It is less versatile, but also a little less prone to cliché than "fire.")
3. House (A third key word. Again, it can be used in different ways in different part of speech.)
4. Never (A more common word. However, it is a negative and will lend an air of sadness to the poem.)
5. And (A very common word. This will help me to construct my lines. At some point, however, if I use this word, one stanza will have to flow grammatically into the next one.)
6. Was (Another common word. I'm hoping that the past tense will increase the air of sadness to the point perhaps even of elegy.)

I don't know exactly how I feel about the fire that nearly burned down my house. It was the first home that I owned, and I had to evacuate. There were a few days when the local media reported that it had been destroyed, but then I found out that my neighborhood had been saved.

I have a lot of complicated emotions about the entire incident, but as a poet, I don't have to have an exact understanding of how I feel or what direction I should take this poem. The form of the poem will do that for me.

You can do the same thing with a moment in your life. The form of the poem is going to take you somewhere. Also, as you go through and you feel that one word or another is not working, change it. No big deal.

By the way, you can also use the six words that I've listed above. See what happens.

As you develop as a sestina writer, try to drop the easier words for more key words and more impact.

Another Newspaper Exercise

Read the news in print or online until you find a story that captures your attention. Start free association. This is an old trick where you think of a subject, any subject, and you just start to list the words on a piece of paper that you think of first. If you spend a minute or two writing these down, you should have six good words to work with at the very least.

Tribute to a Novel Exercise

What is your favorite novel? What are its themes? What are its ideas? What are the key words that you associate with it? In this sestina, you are going to write your tribute to your favorite novel, developing the end words from the themes, ideas and characters in the novel. What did you love about that novel? Chances are it touched something inside of you at just the right moment in your life. Try to give your readers that experience.

Take My Words Exercise

Following are lists of a six words. See if you can work these into poems.

1. men, shame, help, different, run, after
2. insomnia, early, up, house, over, thinking
3. California, rain, change, car, hear, is

Here's another example from Stephanie Barbe Hammer

Listening to Bob Inglis of South Carolina talk to NPR, November 27th 2010

"You lost, Congressman Inglis," says the Interviewer.
"You've blasted your own Republican Party."
Ingliss replies: "But we've been saying things that aren't true.
We've called the Democratic President an illegal immigrant,
A crypto-Muslim, and a Communist. It's simply wrong.
Call me a moron, but I won't tell lies, just to get re-elected,

"And now I'm in a small fraternity who didn't get re-elected."
He laughs softly – his voice gentler than the Interviewer's.
"These folks with their Hummers who shoot moose and elk
        from planes: it's wrong.
Remember – we belong to Teddy Roosevelt's party!
A square deal for everyone including legal immigrants –
We've lost our way somehow, turned from our country's
        original truth."

"Just a minute," says the NPR man. "Aren't you telling the
        truth
Rather belatedly Congressman? And now that you've lost the
        election
Isn't it clear that your moderate mode isn't going to migrate
Inwards or outwards? You haven't convinced anyone," says
        the Interviewer
"And it's clear that you don't have a home now in your own
        party.
So where do you reside exactly, politically-speaking? – am I
        wrong

"To say you're homeless? A politico sleeping in the alley of
        Wrong Way Lane
In a borrowed sleeping-bag?" "Yes," says Inglis. "But at least
        I'm telling the truth
And the truth will out, though it take time and years. My party
Was the party of Lincoln, the party of the Founding Fathers;
        they got elected
On the basis of a vision and that vision still holds." "What?"
        says the interviewer.
"The vision of the American Revolution," answers Inglis.
        "We are all migrants

"In that great journey. We're struggling –not slouching –
        towards that migration
Into justice, freedom, responsible citizenship. We do wrong
When we bend that road to suit our narrow purposes – You

82

see Mr. Interviewer --

I'm sending out a signal here; we all, as leaders, need to see
        the truth

And speak it, regardless of affiliation. This is bigger than re-
        election --

We need to really build consensus between the different
        Parties.

"We've become the Robespierres of our own party --

We treat everyone like a potential traitor or an illegal
        immigrant

If they don't toe the Terror line. To talk about ecology is to
        doom re-election,

But Conservatives *conserve* – that's what the word means!
        Don't get me wrong:

I vote against big government, but we have to raise taxes –
        that's the truth;

The Rich will get no loopholes from me, Mr. Interviewer.

"It's wrong the way we wear out the guillotine on each other's
        party.

We demolish our system with untruths: the president is **not**
        an illegal immigrant

Or a Muslim." "Gosh," says the Interviewer at last. "Too bad
        you didn't get re-elected."

One Last Note

There are many more different types of formal poems out there. Now that you have the feel for how to write in form, developing skills in other forms shouldn't be terribly difficult. Even better, you can create your own forms and help to develop new meanings. Remember that poetry writing should be fun. It can be intellectual game play for adults that results sometimes in something with universal meaning.

About the Author

John Brantingham is a poet and author of literary fiction from Southern California. His work has appeared on Garrison Keillor's daily show, *Writer's Almanac*, and he has had more than 100 poems and stories published in the United States and England in magazines such as *The Journal, Confrontation, Mobius,* and *Tears in the Fence.* His books include *The Green of Sunset, Let Us All Pray Now to Our Own Strange Gods,* and *East of Los Angeles.*

He is a professor at Mt. San Antonio College in Walnut, teaches classes at Northwest Institute of Literary Arts, and leads free camping and writing workshops at Sequoia and Kings Canyon National Parks. He is the writer-in-residence at the dA Center for the Arts in Pomona and the president of the San Gabriel Valley Literary Festival, a non-profit that brings free classes and readings to the San Gabriel Valley. He is one of the fiction editors of *The Chiron Review*, a nationally distributed literary magazine, and he and his wife Annie live happily east of Los Angeles.

About the Series

As actual charcoal provides the artist with a simple, elegant means with which to bring their vision to the canvas, Spout Hill's Charcoal Series of books aims to give writers concise and clear access to the tools needed to meet their academic and creative writing needs. We hope these guides, published in collaboration with leading authors and educators, will serve writers of all ages in perfecting and honing their craft.